- Successful Dating -

No More Frogs
Gemini

21 May – 20 June

by
Cathrine Dahl

CONTENTS

- Successful Dating -
No More Frogs

by Cathrine Dahl

No More Frogs - Successful Dating is your one-stop dating guide. No unnecessary blah-blah. The information is right here, at your fingertips.

This guide can be used in several ways. It's a handy tool when you want to prepare yourself a little. It can give you an advantage when going on a date or getting to know someone you've just met - or even someone you've known for a while.

Although this guide can help you angle your approach, remember to be true to yourself. Have fun, be wise, follow your heart - and keep your feet on the ground!

- Cathrine Dahl

Preface:
A few words about compatibility, and why compatibility guides can give you the wrong idea.

So you've met this Gemini you really, really like, but you're a Scorpio, and the compatibility guides say you're a lousy match. Guess what? That's rubbish!

Some compatibility guides offer a very simplistic approach, claiming that your best matches are the star signs within the same element as you:

Fire: Aries, Leo and Sagittarius
Earth: Taurus, Virgo and Capricorn
Air: Gemini, Libra and Aquarius
Water: Cancer, Scorpio and Pisces

Other guides are slightly more specific, declaring that we are compatible with star signs within our astrological polarity.

Yin: Taurus, Virgo, Capricorn, Cancer, Scorpio and Pisces
Yang: Aries, Leo, Sagittarius, Gemini, Libra and Aquarius

Doesn't look too good, does it? The most optimistic approach has removed half of the population from your dating pool. It doesn't make any sense. The true picture is far more promising...

One star sign, two very different personalities

Each of us has a unique astrological thumbprint determined by the sun, the moon and the planets. The most important factors being your ascending star (ascendant), the sun (star sign) and the moon (feelings).

Let's make it simple
Imagine your star sign being a melody. All the other aspects (the unique positioning of the moon and the planets) are sound effects, applied by a producer with a mixer.

The combination of rhythm, depth and base creates your unique sound. Another person with the same star sign will get his own sound mix and end up with a different beat.

Your personal melody can create wonderful harmonies with star signs you're not supposed to get on with – and nothing but noise with signs that are meant to be matches. You won't find out until you get to know each other.

Let's get to know your date...

THE MALE

YOUR DATE: GEMINI
21 May–20 June

The Essence of him

Convincing – enthusiastic – social – kind – fast-paced – individualistic – smart – eloquent – superficial – restless – able to multitask – impatient – easily distracted – needs people around him– seeks inspiration and input – loves traveling and exploring new turf – has a dualistic personality – dynamic – boyishly charming – attentive – open-minded

...and remember: This is a restless guy who is easily bored. He's always moving forward and needs constant inspiration in order to thrive.

Blind Date – speedy essentials

Who's waiting for you?

That guy over there – yes, the one who's already talking to a couple of other women – either ones he has just met, or a couple of his girlfriends. However, as soon as he sees you, the other women will disappear from his mind. Now he's totally focused on you – well, as long you manage to hold his attention. This shouldn't be a problem, because this is a curious guy who is very interested in people. He's kind, but also restless, both physically and mentally. If you're not used to fast-paced mental activity, he may come across as a little hasty. But hasty or not, this is a very entertaining guy.

Emergency fixes for embarrassing pauses

Embarrassing pauses? Forget it. This man can talk about several things at the same time without losing track of any of them. He will expect you to follow along as he leaps from one subject to the other. He loves interesting news and sassy gossip. If you've got a good story up your sleeve, tell it and you'll have his full attention.

Your place or mine?

The Gemini man is not fixated on sex. However, if the situation should arise... then sure, why not? He is just as impulsive about sex as he is about everything else. But in his world, love and sex are not necessarily connected. Sex on the first date doesn't ensure a call the next day. This man is an expert when it comes to casual hook-ups.

Checklist, before you dash out to meet him:

Keep an open mind, with no fixed expectations
(hint: Don't make him feel cornered)
Prepare ideas about things to do and places to go
(hint: Keep it interesting)
Maintain a positive self-image
(hint: Don't be put off by competition)
Don't dwell on recent break-ups
(hint: Be sparkling and playful)
Know some good stories and fun facts
(hint: Be entertaining)

Tip: This is a fast-moving guy – especially mentally . You'll need to be on your toes to keep up with him. Hold his attention with interesting facts and good stories.

CHAPTER 1

PREPARE YOURSELF

Catch his eye, capture his attention
Top 10 attention grabbers

1. Take the initiative to approach him.
2. Be fun and sparkling. Looking good is not enough.
3. Be playful and show affection – without getting clingy.
4. Impress him with your knowledge.
5. Be outgoing and chat charmingly with other men.
6. Suggest going somewhere fun.
7. Don't be shy about erotic topics.
8. Spark his curiosity by talking about something exotic.
9. Don't be too obvious about your interest. Make him wonder.
10. Offer him a little gossip. He likes it, although he may not admit it.

The SHE. The woman!

The Gemini man is looking for a companion. He wants someone who can join him along the journey of life; someone who is open-minded and embraces everything life has to offer; someone who can inspire him – inside and outside the bedroom! Restless by nature, he doesn't have the patience to sit around and wait for his dream woman to arrive. He is impulsive and gets carried away by interesting women.

The Essence of her

Spontaneous – strong – independent – interesting, never boring – represents a challenge – intelligent –adaptable – fun and humorous – has a positive attitude about life – erotically liberated – enthusiastic – outgoing and social – well-informed, with her own views – entertaining – not afraid of voicing her opinions – attractive

Gemini arousal meter

From 0 to 100... In 10, 15, 20 minutes … if his thoughts are all over the place, he may need a while to focus.

Remember: Be true to yourself

It doesn't matter if he is the most stunning guy you've ever met – if you don't match, you don't match. You may be able to put on a show for a while to hold his attention, but what's the point? We can't please everybody. We all have different needs, dreams, tastes and preferences. There's no such thing as a one-size-fits-all lover. Be yourself, and be true to who you are – always!

Very important: Don't get too comfy in his company. He will lose interest if you start taking it for granted. Make an effort.

CHAPTER 2

THE FIRST DATE

Getting your foot in the door
The basics

Beauty *and* **brains.** Looks are important, but they're not everything. You may have a hard time catching this guy if you're used to relying on your appearance. He may show interest, but if you've got nothing more to offer, he'll be off.

Be stimulating. He prefers engaging women that he can have a discussion with.

Better catch him before he's gone. Don't wait for him to make the first move. This is a popular guy, and if you don't take the initiative, someone else will. Be charming, enthusiastic and entertaining.

Show an interest. As soon as you've got his attention, pick up on his interests and start talking about them.

Don't be shy, be smart. He likes smart women who impress him with knowledge about art, music and what's going on.

Dish a little gossip. He likes gossip because it brings a touch of sensation, so juicy stories are good, too – but steer clear of the negative ones.

Whatever you do...

- **DON'T** rely on a sexy outfit to get his attention.

- **DON'T** be loud and aggressive.

- **DON'T** be too conservative in your ways (manners, etc.).

- **DON'T** be argumentative and fixed in your opinions.

- **DON'T** give the impression you are erotically inhibited.

Remember,
Although he may seem very interested, never take his interest for granted.

- **DON'T** refuse to taste a certain food because you may

not like it.

- **DON'T** be negative or critical.

- **DON'T** interrupt him. Listen and pay attention.

- **DON'T** be clingy. Give him space.

- **DON'T** get jealous when he chats with other women.

If he gets bored, he'll cut and run.

Signs you're in - or not

It can be tricky to figure out where you stand with this man, simply because he's so charming – to everybody. He may go out with you, have a great time and even sleep with you if the mood turns hot and steamy, but none of that guarantees that he's really into you. If you don't manage to trigger his curiosity, he will move on to the next female adventure in his life. This may sound like a challenge, but it doesn't have to be. Just be smart about it. If he's keen on getting to know you further, the signs will be clear:

Chances are he will...

- approach you with charm and boyish enthusiasm
- talk positively about you to others when you're out with him
- ask for your opinion and leave decisions up to you
- make an effort to please you
- call you just to chat
- be more interested in hanging out with you than his friends

Not your type? Making an exit

Getting rid of a Gemini? No problem at all. This freedom-loving, adventure-seeking free spirit will say goodbye as soon as there's a hint of boredom in the air. He believes that life is for living, exploring and enjoying, and remaining in a stagnant relationship is against the fundaments of his nature. It would make him miserable – and he is not a man to hang around and sulk. He very much takes ownership of his own happiness and will quickly move on if things aren't working out.

Exceptions to the rule are rare. It could be that you have dazzled him so much that he has lost touch with reality. He could lack initiative, feel too comfortable or be hoping that he can change you. But if his constant need for speed is driving you nuts, it's time to get the message through.

Foolproof exit measures:

These suggestions will make him go 'What?!' You may want to add a little extra passion, just to make sure it sinks in – and it probably will...!

- Be jealous of everyone. Text him constantly to ask where he is.
- Make sure to be the centre of attention when you're out with friends.
- Criticize his ideas and tell him to be more thorough
- Insist on having sex with the lights out – and no sassy stuff, please!
- Restrict his freedom by demanding that he spend more time with you.
- Tell him to stop flirting when he's being friendly to other women.

CHAPTER 3

SEX'N STUFF

Seductive moves:
How to get him in the mood:

It would probably be easier to figure out what he doesn't like to do in bed – this guy is more or less into anything. His motto is: 'I'll try anything once, and twice if I like it!' ...and he usually does. Any suggestion that's a little out of the ordinary, or comes at a surprising time, will bring a sparkle to his eyes.

Preferences and erotic nature

The Gemini man will have sex anywhere. He's not an inhibited guy, and the chances of being seen can actually increase his excitement. He'll try all sorts of things to bring new angles to his sex life: from positions to gadgets to locations. Be straightforward with him – he will appreciate that. If there are sexual activities you don't enjoy, let him know and he will immediately come up with several different suggestions. This man is serious about pleasing; failure to do so is not an option in his world. In fact, he loves asking his partner to please herself while he watches her. However, this only works if she's ready for it. If she is shy, he will try something else.

Hitting the right buttons

Although every sign has areas on the body that are more sensitive than others, individual sensitivity may vary quite a bit. Don't go body-blind. Honing in on these erogenous zones and forgetting the rest of him is not a good idea. Use these areas to create sparks while turning him on, and as a passion-booster when things get heated. Watch his body language – including the most obvious of signs. Open your mind to the sensuality of touch and taste.

Key areas
Hands and fingers

Get it on
When you shake his hand, be aware that you are touching a part of his body that sends erotic signals to his brain. Depending on the situation, you can actually accomplish a lot through simple hand contact. But remember, this man can be ready on short notice. Don't indicate erotic interest if you don't intend to see it through.

Arouse him
Whenever you touch his hands and fingers, use warm, tender and sensual movements. How? Easy. If you want to arouse him in public, let your hands and fingers 'accidentally' brush against his. If you want to let him know that you have other things in mind than conversation, carefully scratch his hands and fingers with your fingernails – and don't forget the skin between his fingers. Gentle kisses and a brush with the tip of your tongue should make him start to breathe a little quicker...

Surprise him

If you're usually not too vocal in bed, catch him off-guard by whispering a few naughty suggestions into his ear. This will always make him hot – and no need to be particularly creative. The sheer seductiveness of your voice will do the trick.

Spice it up

Bring mirrors into the bedroom. This is a visual guy, and he will get a kick out of exploring you from different angles all at once.

Remember: Although he may come across as erotic and adventurous, he will never want to do anything his partner doesn't appreciate.

His expectations

Expect a lot of energy. He is all about activity, interest and initiative!

Never take it easy. There is no such thing as lying back and expecting a Gemini man to run the show. A passive woman will never excite him.

Keep an open mind. He appreciates someone who is open to new ideas, and who doesn't criticize him when he comes up with new and 'interesting' suggestions.

Lights on, please. He is visually driven, and having sex with the lights out removes an important aspect of his lovemaking. Don't be surprised if he suggests adding a few mirrors around the room.

Playful triggers. You don't have to be an erotic expert to please him. A playful, open and enthusiastic partner will bring out the best in him.

Aims to please. He really wants to be regarded as a good lover. He will work hard to please you – but he will expect you to do the same if you want to keep him around.

Your sensual preferences
Quiz yourself and find out whether this man is for you.

Where on the scale are you?
1 = Don't agree | 3 = Sure | 5 = Agree!

1. Sex can be enjoyed on its own merit, and not only as an expression of romantic feelings.
One a scale for 1 to 5, you are: 1 - 2 - 3- 4 - 5

2. New ideas are important for maintaining a satisfying sex life.
One a scale for 1 to 5, you are: 1 - 2 - 3- 4 - 5

3. In order to fully enjoy sex, the visual aspect is very important.
One a scale for 1 to 5, you are: 1 - 2 - 3- 4 - 5

4. Too much closeness and intimacy can ruin the excitement of sex.
One a scale for 1 to 5, you are: 1 - 2 - 3- 4 - 5

Score 15–20: This will be an ongoing erotic adventure – never boring and always satisfying.
Score 10–14: He may surprise you with unusual suggestions, but that's one of the things that makes sex with him so exciting.
Score 5–9: You may find him a bit too body-focused at times. Let him know what you like. He wants to please his partner – provided your interests are compatible.
Score 1–4: If his playful creativity doesn't knock you off your feet in pleasure, it may send you running for the door.

CHAPTER 4

GENERAL STUFF

The big picture

Keep in mind that the characteristics of a Gemini may vary quite a bit depending on where within the sign he was born, as well as a wide range of additional astrological factors. But for now, let's stick to the basics. Just remember: don't jump to conclusions as soon as you meet him. Give him room to shine. Get to know the man behind the sign.

His personality: Pros and cons

Pros	Cons
• Boyish	• Restless
• Charming	• Superficial
• Dynamic	• Emotionally reserved
• Social	• Indecisive
• Smart	• Has superficial relationships
• Eloquent	• Conflict-avoidant
• Persuasive	• Afraid of romantic commitment
• Enthusiastic	• Blunt
• Individualistic	• A flirt and a player
• Kind	• Impatient
• Supportive	• Has a low threshold for criticism
• Playful	• Doesn't see things through
• Positive	• Ignores negative feedback
• Constructive	• Drifts from one thing to another

Tip: How to show romantic interest

Be sparkling, make an effort to learn about the things he is interested in and keep him wondering how you really feel about him – at least until the time is right.

Romantic Vibes

Mr Gemini:
The enthusiastic and restless partner

The essence

Embrace love. The Gemini man seldom thinks twice about entering into a relationship if a woman has sparked his romantic interest. He expects her to be just as charming and mentally stimulating as the first time he met her. He will leave as soon as he starts getting bored.

Freedom and trust. He really dislikes jealous women. His ideal partner must never criticize him for having female friends or get angry when he flirts.

From love to logic. His feelings are governed by his mind, not his heart. If the relationship starts to close in on him, he will transform his romantic feelings into logical thoughts and find a way to make an exit.

Her pleasure, my command. He is an exciting partner who will turn the world upside down in order to please his woman.

Don't outshine him. He would be insulted if his woman got all the attention. She must shine, but allow him to take centre stage.

Tip: How to show erotic interest

Tell him about an article you've just read about positions that are supposed to increase pleasure during sex. Just let him know you thought it was quite interesting...

Erotic Vibrations

Mr Gemini:
The adventurous and playful lover

The essence

Fun and adventure. He is a restless lover with a playful twinkle in his eyes. This is a smart guy, and he knows exactly how to seduce a woman – even if she's a little shy.

No sweaty sessions. Intense passion is not really his thing. He's interested in performance and excitement, but that does not make him a cold and insensitive lover – far from it.

Adding spice. He is adventurous and always willing to try something new. Don't be surprised if you find a few gadgets and sex toys in his bedroom.

Skip the boring stuff. Traditional lovemaking tends to bore him after a while, and he may come up with new suggestions.

Indecisive... His slightly split personality applies to his sex life, as well. A part of him wants to explore sex without commitment. The other side longs for a more stable life and a long-term partner.

Erotic fun. If you have just met him and are serious about him, be careful. Although he may seem sincere about you, he may also be off first thing the next morning. However, if you just want to have some erotic fun, go for it!

CHAPTER 5

COMPATIBILITY QUIZ

Are you banging your head against the wall, or does he unleash your positive potential? Do you provoke him or bring out the best in him? Does he make you throw your arms up in exasperation, or do you feel inspired and complete in his company? Are the two of you headed towards doom or dream? Take the test to find out.

Question 1.
Do you enjoy having lots of things going on, or do you prefer to focus on one thing at the time?

A. Doing things thoroughly is very important to me – and that's impossible if you have too much going on.
B. I enjoy doing several things at once, but I admit that I'm not always that focused.
C. I need activity to thrive. I have no problem focusing on a few things simultaneously.

Question 2.
Summer is just around the corner , but your budget is limited. How will you spend your vacation?

A. I'd always try to experience and explore something new – no matter what my budget might be.
B. In the peace and quiet, camping somewhere nearby.
C. A staycation could be fun – exploring the area, the neighbourhoods and all the things I've been meaning to do for a long time.

(cont.)

Question 3.
You're having dinner at your Gemini's place. How do you respond when the doorbell rings and you hear him say: 'Tom! Peter! I haven't seen you in ages! Come in! Come in!'?

A. I like doing things at the spur of the moment, and it would be nice to meet his friends. We could always do a romantic dinner another day.
B. What? That is so insensitive. I'd put on my coat and leave.
C. Just typical ... I wouldn't be thrilled, but his spontaneity is also one of the things I find attractive about him.

Question 4.
Do you think it's important to have constant variation in your sex life?

A. I don't want my sex life to be hectic, but I don't want it to become a boring routine, either. I like a nice balance.
B. Absolutely! Having an exciting sex life provides me with renewed energy.
C. The constant quest for new sexual pleasures wears me out. I prefer calm and quiet sex.

Question 5.
In a relationship, do you get jealous?

A. No, not at all.
B. Very seldom.
C. Yes. I'd never tolerate my boyfriend spending time with female friends.

Question 6.
What do you usually do when you run into a problem?

A. Start worrying.
B. Face the issue head-on and find a solution.
C. Call a friend and ask for advice and assistance.

Question 7.
Do you tend to get carried away by enthusiastic ideas?

A. No. I'm very focused, and I keep my feet on the ground.
B. Sometimes, but only if the topic really captures my interest.
C. Absolutely! Any new idea could be a major success just waiting to happen.

Question 8.
Do you find it boring to take turns pleasing each other during sex?

A. Depends on my mood, really. Sometimes I prefer straight-to-the-point sex.
B. Not at all. By taking turns, you really get to enjoy each other.
C. Yes. I'm more into the sensual side of sex, where things are more mutual.

Question 9.
Do you tend to be shy in bed?

A. Not at all. I actually prefer to make love with the lights on.
B. Maybe a little, if the relationship is still new.
C. Yes. I'm a little body-conscious.

Question 10.
Do you find it easy to talk about sex?

A. Why would you want to talk about sex? Sex should be explored and enjoyed physically, not verbally.
B. Yes, provided that the setting is right. There's a time and place for everything.
C. Yes. I love talking about sex. It inspires me.

SCORE	A	B	C
Question 1	1	5	10
Question 2	10	1	5
Question 3	10	1	5
Question 4	5	10	1
Question 5	10	5	1
Question 6	1	10	5
Question 7	1	5	10
Question 8	5	10	1
Question 9	10	5	1
Question 10	1	5	10

75 – 100

Bliss – but not in the traditional, lackadaisical sense of the word. You don't spend the days gazing into each other's eyes. You're out there, living, exploring, enjoying and creating a bond between two individualists. He makes you shine. You inspire him and bring out his potential . The communication between you is unique: with a quick glance across a room full of people, you know exactly what he's thinking. If he's not you dream man, he comes pretty close. Enjoy!

51 – 74

Although he does wear you out from time to time, he still creates an aura of happiness around you. He brings your days to life and fills them with excitement. Neither of you wants a relationship that requires you to spend every minute in each other's company – but you seem to spend a lot of time together anyway. This is partiall because you share the same values and expectations – as well as the joy of exploring new horizons. Boredom will never be an issue for you two. Although you may stumble from time to time, you will learn from each other and continue to grow. Embrace the journey.

26 – 50

How much are you prepared to sacrifice? Are you strong enough to keep your cool when Mr Gemini takes off and doesn't call you for a week? Are you sure this is the man you want in your life, or are you confusing love with excitement? Sure, he's charming, good-looking and fun. He brings energy to your life and makes you feel alive. But does he really satisfy you? Are your most important needs being fulfilled? Love can conquer all, but are you sure this is worth it? It's important to find the right balance. If you feel like one of you is surfing through life while the other is waiting on the beach, something is definitely missing. Be true to yourself and go looking for a man who puts your needs first.

10 – 25

How could two so completely different people end up in each other's company? This is surely one of life's greatest mysteries. Maybe it's a classic case of 'opposites attract', or maybe he touched something within you that made you experience life differently? But the same qualities that struck you as exciting a while ago may now seem like a hassle – for both of you. Perhaps you find him restless and superficial, and he wants you to be more flexible and impulsive. You're pulling in opposite directions and holding each other back. It's time to explore happiness elsewhere.

Thoughts...
Sometimes we have to make an effort, open up and give a little.

Challenges could be opportunities for the relationship to improve and get stronger.

THE FEMALE

YOUR DATE: GEMINI
21 May–20 June

The Essence of her

Impulsive – a quick decision-maker – charming – lively – inventive – likeable – enjoys making things happen – loves luxury in all facets of life – sensually intuitive – assertive – a good multitasker – outgoing and loves socialising – optimistic – a free spirit – influential – positive and constructive – open-minded

...and remember: She is always on the move, either in her mind or out in the world. New experiences feed her energy and enthusiasm for life.

Blind Date – speedy essentials

Who's waiting for you?
She will be smiling and probably wearing something eye-catching; wonderful colours, a bold design or unique accessories. She will be eager to meet you and buzzing with energy. If you're late, she will probably be talking with somebody already. She enjoys people and is very sociable. Whatever shyness she may feel initially will disappear as soon as the two of you start talking. She will radiate enthusiasm and positivity – provided her date isn't holding back and being too serious.

Emergency fixes for embarrassing pauses.
If you manage to make her sit in silence, you will have either utterly dazzled her with your looks and charm or turned her off completely. If you make a lousy impression, she won't stay long. On the other hand, if she really likes you, you can loosen her up with fun stories, innocent gossip and interesting facts. It won't take long before she's back to her sparkling self.

Your place or mine?
Whichever is the most convenient. The Gemini woman loves adventure and may easily be seduced into having sex on a first date. However, you'll need to be careful. If you really like her but fail to satisfy her in bed, she won't return your call the next day. She needs her man to be on the same level as she is, both mentally and physically. Merely a quick burst of passion will probably turn her off.

Checklist, before you dash out to meet her:

Have a few interesting facts or stories ready
(hint: Entertain her)
Wear a stylish outfit and a few expensive accessories
(hint: Be classy)
Make reservations at a nice place
(hint: She loves luxury)
Have some creative ideas, like getting a massage at a spa
(hint: Pamper her)
Be well-groomed, minding your face hands and hair
(hint: No scruffiness)

Tip: Never underestimate her. Although she may demonstrate a naïve femininity, she's very smart. If you fail to appreciate this, she will probably move on quickly.

CHAPTER 1

PREPARE YOURSELF

Catch her eye, capture her attention
Top 10 attention grabbers

1. Wear a stylish outfit and maintain an aura of masculinity.
2. Show her your charming personality.
3. Exhibit a confident and friendly attitude towards people around you.
4. Demonstrate generosity and pamper her.
5. Make intelligent comments and ask interesting questions.
6. Wear a big smile.
7. The Gemini woman will appreciate assertiveness and taking the initiative to try something new.
8. Exude playful boyishness, while keeping your feet on the ground.
9. Show off a luxury item, like a stylish car.
10. Be impulsive – surprise her.

The HE. The man!

The Gemini woman wants a little bit of everything. Her man needs to be strong, masculine and caring, but not possessive or restrictive of her freedom. He must be adventurous and free-spirited, but never make her feel insecure. He must be playful and energetic, but still responsible and reasonable. It's a tall order, and all about finding the right balance.

The Essence of him

Flexible in his views – tolerant – liberal and open-minded – strong and masculine, but not too body-focused – good-looking and well-dressed – adventurous – creative in bed – playful and enthusiastic – entertaining in social setting – protective and caring – generous – with a fondness for the good things in life – intelligent– optimistic – has a good sense of humour

Gemini arousal meter
From 0 to 100... In 10 minutes, provided you have managed to spark her imagination, or responded to an erotic suggestion with enthusiasm.

Remember: Be true to yourself

It doesn't matter if she is the most stunning girl you've ever met – if you don't match, you don't match. You may be able to put on a show for a while to hold her attention, but what's the point? We can't please everybody. We all have different needs, dreams, tastes and preferences. There's no such thing as a one-size-fits-all lover. Be yourself, and be true to who you are – always!

Very important: If you ask for her opinion, make sure to pay attention. If you come back with the same problem the next day, she will look at you strangely and wonder why you didn't get the point the first time.

CHAPTER 2

THE FIRST DATE

Getting your foot in the door
The basics

Excite and inspire. She needs new experiences to thrive. Men who fail to inspire her won't stand a chance. She may be charming and polite for a while, but it won't last. Hold onto her attention by being interesting.

Ask for her advice. She is a keen listener and will always give you her opinion.

Engage and fascinate. Brush up on your knowledge about all sorts of things: culture, politics and even gossip. People born under this sign enjoy a bit of gossip.

A luxury... Take her out to an expensive restaurant. She loves luxury and her conversation flows naturally over a glass of champagne. Don't be a cheapskate! Giving her a gift? Try something unusual. When in doubt, a luxurious item by a famous brand will usually be a hit.

Don't hold back. She loves intellectual and active people. Show your adventurous, dynamic, spontaneous and exciting sides – well, maybe not all at the same time...

Whatever you do...

• **DON'T** ask her to split the bill.

• **DON'T** come on too strong.

• **DON'T** choose the cheapest items on the menu.

• **DON'T** forget to compliment her ideas.

• **DON'T** talk about boring everyday topics.

Remember, she expects you to be just as energetic and impulsive as she is. Don't get lazy and

- **DON'T** forget your manners and start knocking back food and drink.

- **DON'T** underestimate her by asking silly questions.

- **DON'T** be pessimistic.

- **DON'T** criticise her opinions or tell her to face reality.

- **DON'T** be too absorbed in yourself and your own views.

make her take the lead. Everything needs to be mutual, or she will lose interest.

Signs you're in - or not

If she likes you, she will show it. She seldom waits for the guy to make the first move. Her philosophy is: If you want something, go for it! Why waste precious time just staring at the phone and hoping he will call? She'd much rather get a 'no' than keep wondering. And deep down, she doesn't expect you to say no! Her intuition is good, and she usually has a feel for whether a guy is interested or not. If you're not sure about her intentions, look for these signals:

Chances are she will...

- be the first to call and text after a date, and she will always text you back right away
- invite you to an exhibition, a special party or something similar
- get you a gift based on something you've talked about
- make room in her life to see you frequently
- take an interest in your interest
- share her sensual thoughts and ideas...

Not your type? Making an exit

Getting out of a relationship with a Gemini woman is easy – very easy. She is a free spirit, always on the move and searching for inspiration, ideas and adventures. She needs a man who can keep up with her and preferably lead the way from time to time. She sees life as too precious to be wasted on boring relationships. She needs energy and excitement, and craves a man who is dynamic and spontaneous. Her life is for living – and loving someone who shares her values.

If things aren't working out, she will probably be the first to go. She has a very low tolerance for miserable situations. However, if she has fallen for you completely, or if she's too busy to notice that you're no longer fascinated by her, it will be up to you to wake her up to reality.

Foolproof exit measures:

Make sure you really want to break up with her before you go ahead these measures – because when she's gone, she's gone.

- Stop taking her seriously and begin to question her ideas
- Take her camping and sleep in a dirty tent
- Reduce sex to a once-a-week, under-the-covers event
- Criticize her for spending money on pointless luxury
- Be selfish, and start sulking and complaining about everything
- Act indifferent about your looks, including the way you dress

CHAPTER 3

SEX'N STUFF

Seductive moves:
How to get her in the mood:

The Gemini woman is impulsive, flexible and tolerant, and turning her on – or at least sparking her erotic interest – is quite easy. But don't take her sexual interest for granted. If she suspects you're only looking for a quick one before going to sleep, she will probably suggest making you a mug herbal tea instead. This woman is no sleep aid.

Preferences and erotic nature
She loves men with a taste for adventure – including in the bedroom. New, erotic suggestions excite her. As a playful lover, she appreciates anything that can make her sex life more exciting, including sex toys. Don't be surprised if she suddenly pulls out a couple of interesting-looking, vibrating items. A man who can expand her horizons without being too kinky makes her tingle . He must be creative and respect her assertiveness and need for change – including her sensual suggestions. A traditional man-on-top guy won't remain in her bedroom for long. Foreplay is also important to a Gemini woman. And if her partner uses his creativity when touching her, she will respond with increasing passion...

Hitting the right buttons

Although every sign has areas on the body that are more sensitive than others, individual sensitivity may vary quite a bit. Don't go body-blind. Honing in on these erogenous zones and forgetting the rest of her is not a good idea. Use these areas to create sparks while turning her on, and as a passion-booster when things get heated. Watch her body language – including the most obvious of signs. Open your mind to the sensuality of touch and taste.

Key areas
Her arms, palms and fingers

Get it on
If you were to accidentally brush your fingers over her hands, you might notice a slight flush to her cheeks. The slightest touch to her hands, palms or lower arms might trigger an intimate reaction.

Arouse her
Focus on her hands and fingers. One of the advantages of her erogenous zones is that you can arouse her anywhere you like, without people noticing. However, if you want to move onto the real stuff, you may want to start in the comfort of a private place. This woman simply loves having her hands and fingers sucked, licked, kissed and even bitten. Use your imagination.

Surprise her

Give her a gentle hand massage. Make sure to use lots of cream or oil to allow your hands to slide easily over, and between, her fingers. Finish off by gently caressing her with the tips of your fingers...

Spice it up

Playing erotic games can actually be quite fun – but don't make them too complicated. It will be important not to allow the planning to take the fun and impulsiveness out of it.

Remember: She may have been chasing you, but if you fail to live up to her expectations, she will leave as quickly as she came.

Her expectations

No rush. The Gemini woman's preferences can be summed up very succinctly: She likes anything that is exciting and adventurous – provided you don't rush her into it.

Be prepared. Sex with her is not confined to the bedroom. She's up for having sex in all sorts of unusual places. If the mood arises while the two of you are out driving, she may respond positively to having sex in the backseat of your car – depending on where you are, obviously.

Active and assertive. She is assertive and enjoys being sexually active. Never suggest that she should play more passive role. That will turn her off.

Keep it fun. She usually gets more pleasure from fun and exciting sex than intensely passionate sex. ' Hot and steamy', to her, means a sticky gym.

Try something new. She may suggest having sex simply because she is looking for a new adventure. She'll satisfy her need to explore while you'll get excitement with added erotic pleasure: a win-win situation.

Attentive. No matter what her preferences might be, she will always try hard to please her partner. Very few men will feel disappointed after a night with this amazing woman.

Your sensual preferences
Quiz yourself and find out whether this woman is for you.

Where on the scale are you?
1 = Don't agree | 3 = Sure | 5 = Agree!

1. Playfulness and new ideas are the key to a happy sex life.
One a scale for 1 to 5, you are: 1 - 2 - 3- 4 - 5

2. Sex should never be confined to a certain place or time.
One a scale for 1 to 5, you are: 1 - 2 - 3- 4 - 5

3. A creative and assertive sex partner brings out the passion in me.
One a scale for 1 to 5, you are: 1 - 2 - 3- 4 - 5

4. Impulsiveness is important in order to live out your sensual feelings.
One a scale for 1 to 5, you are: 1 - 2 - 3- 4 - 5

Score.
15 - 20: You both appreciate impulsiveness, adventure and playfulness. This could be fun.
10 - 14: This woman will keep you on your toes, and you like that. Your erotic life will be sparkling.
05 - 09: Her impulsiveness can be a challenge at times, but it may also broaden your erotic horizon.
01 - 04: Does she have a bit too much energy at times? If you cherish quiet, sensual moments, this could be a challenge.

CHAPTER 4

GENERAL STUFF

The big picture

Keep in mind that the characteristics of a Gemini may vary quite a bit depending on where within the sign she was born, as well as a wide range of additional astrological factors. But for now, let's stick to the basics. Just remember: don't jump to conclusions as soon as you meet her. Give her room to shine. Get to know the woman behind the sign.

Her personality: Pros and cons

Pros	Cons
• Creative	• Restless
• Energetic	• Prone to gossip
• Adventurous	• Impatient
• Charming and feminine	• Needs to be liked
• Clever	• Uses her looks to her advantage
• Open-minded	• Maintains shallow relationships
• Sociable and friendly	• Superficial
• Sexually intuitive	• Has low stamina
• A good listener	• Romantically indecisive
• A lover of people	• Antsy
• Playful and enthusiastic	• Fakes luxury with bling
• Attractive	• Hyperactive
• Assertive in bed	• Ignores her own feelings
• Liberated	• Emotionally distant

Tip: How to show romantic interest

Be generous and even a little old-fashioned. She's not one for subtle hints. Flowers, gifts and lots of attention will do the trick ... pamper her and let her know you want to spend more time with her.

Romantic Vibes

Miss Gemini:
The positive and energetic partner

The essence

Embrace life! Life is an adventure, and she embraces every opportunity to explore something new in any part of her life, including in her relationships. She doesn't want a life filled with boring routines. This may be part of the reason that Gemini women often have quite a few relationships before settling down.

Commitment doesn't scare her. She actually looks forward to it. The challenge is finding the right man, someone who shares her enthusiasm for adventure.

Find the right balance. Security is important to her, but too much makes her restless.

A jewel. She is attractive and feminine and will always shine when she's out with her man. She gets a kick out of making him proud.

Enthusiastic. She's interested in all sorts of things and easily becomes inspired to try something new. There's seldom a dull moment in her life.

Emotional space. A little bit of everything. Activity and energy are at the core of her character. Too many romantic evenings at home can make her antsy.

Tip: How to show erotic interest

Easy. All you have to do is make a suggestion. Make it playful and interesting, and avoid being blunt or crude. Be seductive about it. Use your voice and your eyes.

Erotic Vibrations

Miss Gemini:
The playful and creative lover

The essence

Keep it exciting. Don't expect her to be satisfied with missionary position or settle for sex once a week in a dark bedroom. Hold onto her interest by being creative.

A little research... If you're not feeling particularly creative in the sex department, do a little research. Don't introduce anything new unless you know what you are doing. Bringing a textbook to bed will turn her off. A few nice visuals, on the other hand – well, that's a different matter...

Don't rush it. She won't respond well to being pushed. Allow her to set her own pace.

Tune in. Make sure your sensual antennas are perfectly tuned. Her mood can change from super hot to ice cold in two seconds if you fail to interpret her wishes correctly.

A sensual butterfly. Her need for change can sometimes result in her moving from one partner to another – but this will only happen if she's in a casual relationship.

Broaden your horizons. Don't be put off if you get the impression that she's trying to adjust your ways in order to make your sex life more interesting. This can actually be very rewarding and broaden your sexual horizons.

CHAPTER 5

COMPATIBILITY QUIZ

Are you banging your head against the wall, or does she unleash your positive potential? Do you provoke her or bring out the best in her? Is she making you throw your arms into the air in exasperation, or do you feel inspired and complete in her company? Take the test to find out.

Question 1.
Your girlfriend has been giving you erotic hints all evening. How do you react when she suddenly forgets about the whole thing?

A. I don't like that at all. You should finish what you've started – no matter what.
B. No big deal. We'll make up for it soon anyway.
C. It can be a little frustrating, but her impulsiveness is part of what makes her so attractive.

Question 2.
Your girlfriend has surprised you by booking a weekend away for the two of you, attending a fun seminar. How do you respond?

A. This is one of the things I really love about her: she makes life so interesting and exciting.
B. Without asking me about my plans? Inconsiderate.
C. I prefer to plan things myself, but sometimes I do need a kick in the butt.

(cont.)

Question 3.
What does a relaxing weekend look like to you?

A. Sitting in front of the fireplace reading a book.
B. Doing odd jobs around the house during the day; going out and having fun in the evening.
C. Taking off somewhere to experience something new and exciting.

Question 4.
Do you think it's important to try out different things to keep your sex life interesting?

A. I don't want to get stuck in a routine, but I'm not fanatic about trying new things.
B. You only live once. My life, including my sex life, should be exciting.
C. No. I'm not all that into sex. I prefer closeness and tenderness.

Question 5.
Do you mind if your girlfriend has male friends?

A. Not at all. Why should I?
B. It depends on whether I know who they are.
C. Yes. What's wrong with our mutual friends?

Question 6.
How do you feel about a girl who seems more interested in an exciting sex life than tenderness and sensuality?

A. That's fine by me.
B. Not my style at all. I prefer warm and sensual women.
C. I think it's important to have an exciting sex life, but it's equally important to experience intimacy during sex.

Question 7.
Do you regard yourself as creative?

A. Creative? Where's the dictionary?
B. I wouldn't necessarily describe myself as creative, but I've got a vivid imagination.
C. Yes, absolutely.

Question 8.
Do you find it boring to take turns pleasing each other?

A. That depends on my mood. Sometimes, I prefer to just get straight to the point.
B. Not at all; I love it. It gives me a chance to enjoy my partner.
C. Yes. How boring can you get?

Question 9.
How do you feel about independent and professional women?

A. I support traditional gender roles: a man should be a man, and a woman should be by his side.
B. I'm really cool with successful women, provided I still get to feel like a man.
C. No problem at all. I support equal opportunities in every aspect of life.

Question 10.
Are you able to express sexual feelings verbally?

A. Yes! I often whisper naughty nothings into my girlfriend's ear.
B. Verbal sexuality? Is this something new?
C. Yes, but only if I'm in the mood.

SCORE	A	B	C
Question 1	1	10	5
Question 2	10	1	5
Question 3	1	5	10
Question 4	5	10	1
Question 5	10	5	1
Question 6	10	1	5
Question 7	1	5	10
Question 8	5	10	1
Question 9	1	5	10
Question 10	10	1	5

75 – 100

Running out of ideas? Never! Wish there were more hours in the day? Probably! For the two of you, every day is a new adventure waiting to be explored. You seize the moment and embrace every excitement that comes your way. Impulsiveness is at the core of your relationship, and that makes it fun and unpredictable. You will never be bored. The two of you are perfectly matched, no doubt about it. No advice needed. You know exactly how to handle your woman.

51 – 74

Fun and excitement are a major part of your life. Who cares if it can get slightly hectic? You're having a great time. The only thing to watch out for is that you don't start trying new things just for the sake of it. This could make you feel shallow and restless. Make sure to devote time to your deeper feelings, both romantic and sexual. But you've already mastered the joy, adventure and freedom that are the key to her heart; it comes naturally to you and everything seems to be running smoothly. No big issues. No major discussions. Wonderful days ahead.

26 – 50

It may feel like you're stuck at a crossroads. There are several options, but you cannot make up your mind. You long for more depth and stability in your life, but you are also attracted to the impulsiveness and adventure the Gemini woman brings. Still, it can be difficult to keep up with her at times. She's always juggling several tasks at once, whereas you prefer to keep a singular focus. Sometimes you wish she could be a little more thorough, and you know she often wishes she could spur you into action. Both of these are possible. Happiness is within reach. Just be careful not to sacrifice your own needs to fulfill hers. A relationship should be a place for growth, not a battleground.

10 – 25

Why are you holding onto a relationship that gives you so much grief? Chances are, if you don't do anything about it, she will. If your feelings for her are strong, talk to her before it's too late. There are solutions to everything, and you can make it work – if you want to. Life is too short to waste on arguments and disappointments. It's time to be true to yourself and to each other. Your need for comfort, closeness and stability might be impossible to establish with her – but you'll have to talk to her to find out.

Thoughts...
Sometimes, a challenge is what we need in order to grow. However, only accept a challenge for the right reasons. Make sure your heart is in it. Love should be real. Never pretend.

...just a final note:
This book has not been approved by your date and should be treated accordingly. He or she *may* not agree with the content.

www.ingramcontent.com/pod-product-compliance
Lightning Source LLC
Chambersburg PA
CBHW071838020426
42331CB00007B/1770